Mindfulness for Dog Lovers

Wisdom of Dogs, Volume 1

Suzanne Grosser

Published by Suzanne Grosser, 2022.

While every precaution has been taken in the preparation of this book, the publisher assumes no responsibility for errors or omissions, or for damages resulting from the use of the information contained herein.

MINDFULNESS FOR DOG LOVERS

First edition. February 6, 2022.

Copyright © 2022 Suzanne Grosser.

ISBN: 979-8215381748

Written by Suzanne Grosser.

Table of Contents

My Quest

The Goal

I set out to attain mindfulness: that esoteric state of peace and calm where I could exist blissfully in each and every moment of my life.

I expected a soothing practice that would calm my worried mind and relax my bouncy brain.

I hoped to emulate the Tibetan monks I had encountered a decade ago.

Exiled from their home country, they were doing a tour of the United States. A local health food store had cleared the dining area and roped it off to make space for the monks to create a sand mandala. The mandala was nearly 10 feet in diameter. Wearing their brightly colored red and orange robes, they took turns working on the project in groups of three or four. They focused their attention on meticulously shaking bits of colored sand into a beautiful design.

We all knew it would be destroyed at the end of the week.

Some locals stood and watched. Others sat on the floor nearby in silent meditation, giving their energy to the project. I watched for a bit but of course I had errands to run and little time for stillness.

The monks offered music CDs for sale. I decided to buy one to support their work and to help me meditate. Maybe assuage my guilt at running off so quickly. I was about to learn a lesson.

The young man who sold me a CD did not merely take my money and hand me a product in return. He took my money with humbleness and gratitude. He looked, really looked, at me.

He paused as he put the CD in my hand. He did not immediately let go of it. He was not touching me but he forced me to slow down. I didn't want to yank it out of his hands!

I had to pause and wait and recognize that this was a moment where we connected. We looked into each other eyes. We exchanged gifts. Money I could spare. Music he could share.

The mandala creation was mindfulness. But so was that pause. We were both in that moment together. Connecting. Giving and receiving. There was hope in that moment that perhaps if I slowed down, I could connect with others.

I went on with my busy life and quickly got back up to speed. Years went by. I don't even know if you can buy music on CDs anymore! But I never forgot those earnest young eyes. That moment of connection.

Then 2020 Happened

Our ability to connect with others was circumscribed. I thought again of the monks and the aura of present moment awareness and peacefulness that surrounded them.

Granted, in 2020 I thought of a lot of things. Like starting a website to consider the intersection of spiritual wisdom and our family pets. It's called wisdomofdogs.com. (Don't worry, there's a link in the back of the book so you can check it out later)

I decided it was time to explore mindfulness in earnest. With the help of my dogs, of course.

The Method

Normally when I undertake a new venture, I give it 30 days. Theoretically that's how long it takes to develop a new habit. It has not worked for me in the past with meditation, or exercise, or eating more vegetables, or pretty much anything.

So this time, I went on a journey instead. I invited my newsletter subscribers to join me. This book, with some edits for clarity, is a compilation of the reports my subscribers received as I took this journey.

Because I had invited others along, I couldn't just quit. I couldn't slack off. I did miss a few weeks. I'm sure I had good reasons/excuses, but I don't remember what they were now. (Hangs head shamefully.)

Knowing my email list was expecting a report kept me (mostly) on track. If I gave up, I wouldn't only let myself down. Some weeks I was scrambling for a topic. I had to try something! Or share something more personal than I had planned.

Unexpected

I thought mindfulness would bring me calmness, a feeling of peace. It did. But that wasn't all it brought.

I discovered mindfulness brings honesty and a clarity of vision that I had not expected.

My journey morphed from a simple "Oh look I'm paying attention and I feel peaceful" to "Oh look I'm paying attention and this doesn't fit with my life."

Yikes!

It was wasn't all sweetness and calm. But it was worth the trip.

The Result

I am more mindful than when I started. Not nearly as mindfully wise as my dog, but I am on the right track.

Before we start this journey together, I'd like you to meet the dogs who acted as my guides.

My Guides

Sandy

My current canine companion is a mix of Beagle and Yellow Lab, a Beagador if you will. She is possibly the friendliest dog on the planet. She is adorable and knows it. Works it. I am certain that more of my neighbors know her name than know mine. She lives for attention, treats, and good things to sniff.

Tala and Olie

Tala was a Cattle Dog-Collie mix with a sense of humor and strong work ethic. Her littermate Olie was the quiet sister, although the first into the fray if her pack was threatened. Like most herders they were not overly friendly but they did have a select group of humans they loved and would greet eagerly. They watched over me, took on jobs they felt I was neglecting, and amazed me with their ability to take control of any situation.

Huff

Huff was a Border Collie-Aussie mix who came to me late in his life. Our time together was short, only 17 months but we packed a lot of love into those months. He had a sense of humor and a lot of fears. We were made for each other.

Ashes

Ashes was a purebred keeshond. He was a handsome mountain of black, silver and gray fur with a gentle disposition and unending patience. He watched over my children as they grew up and moved on into their own lives.

Making a Start

I'm really going to do it: 2021 is my year of mindfulness.

Let's start at the beginning with what I am trying to achieve.

By mindfulness I mean that state of actually being where I am. Seeing what I see. Hearing what I hear. In the present, fully with the people and things that are here with me. Doing whatever I am doing with my whole self.

Simple for dogs, but pretty much the opposite of what most humans do. I am usually thinking ahead to the next thing on my to-do list. Or stewing over that remark a co-worker made two days ago. Worrying about politics and justice. Hoping for peace.

But never achieving peace in the moment, because I am not present there to receive it.

A Ruff Start

(I know, I know but I love an awful pun.)

As Steven Pressfield warned, any time you are working on a worthwhile project, resistance will show up early and often.

For my 2021 mindfulness practice, resistance showed up right on time: on January 1st .

Resistance pretended to be my logical brain and asked "If you stay in the present how will you plan for the future? There will be no dog treats in the cupboard because you wouldn't bother to make a list and go to the store. There will be no lights in the house because you wouldn't plan ahead to pay the electric bill. Or even get to work on time"

A lot of exaggeration. But hey, that is what resistance does.

It didn't give up: "Sure, mindfulness is okay for monks in a cloister where someone else runs things and worries things but in real life . . ."

I sighed. I've been doing that a lot lately. I promised resistance that I would think over its concerns. And I did. I decided that if resistance is so eager to stop me, this mindfulness thing must be a worthwhile project.

So I continue.

Yoga

Off to an easy start with yoga, a classic mindfulness practice.

But I have a problem with yoga. Yoga is the antithesis of achievement. You move through positions and the end of it, you have observed your breath and tested your body. But you didn't actually accomplish anything. It is not about achieving a pose, but observing what your body can do and how it feels about doing it.

Sandy can do yoga. She will taunt me with her downward facing dog which is much more flexible than mine. When we pass the yoga ladies in the park as they set up their mats, her tail wag is so infectious one or two is will break ranks to pet her. So she demonstrates her "Urdhva Mukha Pasasana" or "thread the needle" pose as she angles for more attention and belly rubs. They fuss over her.

But when I want to yoga at home, she declines. She drops toys on the mat and stretches out taking up the whole space, I am willing to share the mat but really? When it is time for savasana, she has had enough. Why am I lying down, when I could playing tug or going for a walk or making dinner? You can read more about our yoga attempts here at wisdomofdogs.com website.

Yoga, like so many mindfulness practices, is observation not action. Practice, not achievement.

I am uncomfortable with the idea of just being, not doing. I have been trained from childhood to do, to achieve, to accomplish. I was raised as a human doing. I am learning to accept myself as a human being.

I do feel better after yoga. I feel stronger physically, quieter mentally, and calmer emotionally. As a mindfulness practice, it is a win for me. Because it showed me myself: my accomplishment-based achievement-driven human-doing self. Now it is time my being-self.

I will keep doing yoga. And seek out more non-doings.

Lesson 1 from my year of mindfulness:

Be more like my dogs, less like a machine. Be a human being.

Non-doing

In search of my being-self, I made a list of things I did this week that are more being than doing. Here are 3 of them:

1. Watching goldfinches work the bare limbs of the maple tree, finding sustenance in something that looks dead. Such a nice splash of color against the gray winter sky!

1. Walking Sandy. Like most beagles, she is a high maintenance walking companion. It requires my full attention to take evasive action before she gets within striking distance of enticing tidbits. The neighborhood hawks are prone to leave leftovers from their hunts along our path. Bunny turds are also a favorite. NO matter how many times I assure Sandy that we have plenty of food at home and this is not a foraging expedition, her beagle nature is undeniable.

1. Sipping tea on the porch in the morning sunshine. I'm dressed in multiple layers against the cold, cradling my warm mug in my fingerless gloved hands. The birds are singing because they are as happy as I am that the sun is out.

I'm hoping you find your own bits of non-doing.

Play as Non-Doing

If you spend much time with a child, you know that despite the commotion, most of the noise and activity it is actually non-doing.

When I play with my granddaughter, we don't accomplish things. There are no books written or floors cleaned. We play. We have a good time and enjoy each other's company.

We laugh. We use our imagination. We find animals in the cloud. And make up games about captive dragons.

We make art. Well, she makes art. I make – an effort. We do crafts.

Technically, with arts and crafts we are "doing" in that we produce a physical something. But those somethings are not the point. They never were. The point is the shared experience, the being together.

Perhaps this is true of more doings than I realize.

Sandy is giving me her well-duh look! Humans are so slow to learn what dogs already know.

Being Someone Else

Mindfulness is being fully in the present. So is getting lost in the story of a good book mindfulness?

I give this question an unequivocal: sort of.

Usually when I am reading I am also snacking (yeah, yeah, I know.) I read. I sip tea. I pet the dog. This was one of Huff's favorite times. He was too old for rambunctious play but he loved the gentle pets and warmth of snuggling against my leg. I loved that too.

But sometimes, the story sucks me in. The snacking stops. The tea goes cold and the dog curls up to sleep beside me. He knows my attention is elsewhere and the snacks are gone anyway.

On one level, I am not fully in my body. I am not in *my* living room under *my* cozy blanket. I have been transported to another world, but I am fully in that world. My pulse quickens when the heroine is in trouble. I laugh when she is snarky. I cry when her mentor dies. I am not reliving my past or worrying about my future. Her present has become my present. I am fully in the world, but an alternate one.

It's not exactly present moment awareness. But it's not too far away from it either.

Mindful Eating Week 1

This week's goal was mindful eating. It was a total fail!

The Plan

Eat mindfully. Pay attention to each bite. Savor my meals. Actually taste my food. Simple.

Not for me.

Bad Habits

I shovel food like I am going for a world record. I am frequently putting a bite of food in my mouth before I have finished chewing the one before it. Which could be a discussion for the psychiatrist's couch. I could blame my parents if I tried hard enough.

Dullness

I simply don't have sensitive taste buds. I know people who can parse out the individual flavors in a complex soup. When I eat food these folks have prepared for me, I gobble the first two bites at usual. Then it hits me and I stop. "Wow, this is really good!" It is like coming up for air and realizing, "Hey I like breathing."

I try to slow down my eating for these people in deference to their effort to feed me well. Still, it is a struggle. Sigh. I am such a work in progress

Distraction

I like to read when I eat. And there is always something to read. Even if my phone is across the room, and the books are tucked safely away on the shelf, there will be words somewhere on the table – the back of the battery package for instance. Even though it is mostly a list of warnings not to do stupid things like eat the batteries.

Ah-ha – maybe that is why I need to be mindful, so I don't inadvertently eat batteries or other non-edibles.

My Enabler

Sandy is with me on this. She scarfs up her food barely chewing. She is a beagle after all. Such behavior is functional for a pack animal who needs to get their share quickly. But I don't have to fight anyone for my share of the food. And Sandy sometimes does eat things better left alone.

As my enabler, Sandy not only emulates my quick eating habit, she supports it. Because the faster I eat, the quicker we get to the leftover tidbits she is counting on. I know, I know. Don't give your dog table scraps. Honestly, prehistoric dogs didn't start hanging out with humans for our personalities – they liked our leftovers.

I do limit what I give her and adjust her dinner bowl accordingly. But I digress.

My Plan

My plan was to focus on the story behind my food and my reasons for eating. I would consider where it came from and offer gratitude for all those involved in the process of getting that food to my table.

I would think about what my food is doing for my body. Vitamins and proteins and antioxidants and such.

That sort of worked, until I was distracted. Printed words!

Or rushed through it. Bad habits!

Or just plain forgot. My food was gone and thirty minutes later I was trying to remember if I ate and if I did eat, was it good? Sigh.

Mindful Eating Week 2

I failed so badly in week 1, I decided to give myself another week to redeem myself.

I kept trying and a few times did make it through a entire meal paying attention. Damn few.

I felt fuller and more important, satisfied with what I had eaten. Sandy was a little mopey – but life goes on.

I gave it one last attempt. A shortened version of the practice that I might actually get through successfully.

I decided to sit and savor a square of super dark chocolate because It's one of my favorite things.

I thought. Turns out when I take the time to really nibble and chew and loll that deep rich chocolate on my tongue, it's actually quite bitter. I. Don't. Like. It.

I can slowly eat and appreciate super dark, hardly any sugar chocolate. But it turns out I don't want to. Who knew?

Spiritual Lesson from Failure Alert!

The point of savoring and of mindfulness is to appreciate the good things in your life, to feel gratitude, to be in the moment. To enjoy.

Mindfulness might also be about opening your eyes to what you don't like. What you don't want in your life.

Oh dear.

Lessons Learned

I do not like super-dark chocolate.

I do like pasta with a lot of veggies.

There are things I do not want on my plate. And I don't think that applies only to my actual dinner plate.

Accidental Mindfulness

I live in the southern USA, so warm weather comes earlier here than in many parts of the world. As the weather warms, I am drawn outside by the sunshine and the birdsong. Both promise warmer weather on the way.

There is new life bursting out of flower beds and emerging from hibernation burrows. Crocuses and daffodils push through the protective winter mulch. The leaves begin popping out on the maple tree, shading the space where I buried Huff.

I sip my morning tea on the porch enjoying the warm breeze and the gentle morning sun. I did not set out to meditate. But somehow, I am. I am fully in this moment. I am mindful. I am doing it!

Perhaps not trying so hard is the key. Simply relax. Listen. Look. Breathe.

On Pride and Pollen

The other day, a friend asked if I was having trouble with my allergies this season. I blithely replied, "Nope. I'm doing good." I congratulated myself on finally having built up my immunity. At long last, my body has figured out that pollen is not a threat. There is no need to produce copious amounts of nasal fluid and initiate violent bouts of sneezing. I have triumphed!

Pride goeth before a fall, the proverb says.

The next day, *the very next day*, the dogwoods in my neighborhood bloomed. All of them. All at once. A mass orgy of white petaled procreation.

Turns out, I have not built up my immunity.

My body has figured out nothing. My immune system went on high alert when that lovely morning breeze carried the dogwood's pollen to my nose.

In fact, it is much worse this year than normal. I usually power through without meds but not this year. I cycle through antihistamine brands, hoping for one strong enough to let me breathe outside for more than twenty minutes. And still I sneeze and snot. I am tempted to hunker down inside until the yellow plague passes over. Yes, where I live, the proportions are biblical.

But there is Sandy and walks will happen. So out I go, but I pay attention to the flowering things on my route – avoiding the dogwood lined streets, which helps not much. I cannot outwit or outrun the natural forces around me.

If the finger of God writes with pollen, I must pay attention.

Birding

For me birding is the ultimate mindfulness practice. My apologies to those of you who can monitor your breathing and think no other thoughts for 30 minutes or more. That ain't me babe. Honestly those folks threw up their hands in despair about week 3 and are now meditating sending good vibes to me down here in my lowly earth bound existence.

But birding keeps me focused in the here and now. It keeps me where I am, doing what I am doing, and only that.

I don't worry about email, or getting the oil changed in my car. I'm not planning dinner or Sandy's next blog post. That should be her job anyway!

I look for birds. I listen to the sounds from the trees. I watch where I step. This last point is especially important when looking for a bird high up in a tree through your binoculars. You need a better angle. You need to take a step or two backwards. Pro tip: look away from the bird and check the ground behind you before you step.

It is better to survey the terrain with your eyes than your butt. Which is exactly what happens if you don't know there is tree root behind you. Next thing you know, you are on the ground, have lost sight of the bird, and mud is soaking through the seat of your pants.

My point is that mindfulness is absolutely required if you are birding. You have to stay quiet and listen. Watch for rustling leaves, a darting shadow. Notice things like that motionless hawk at the top of snag. He is so well camouflaged, you won't see him if you aren't giving this space your full attention. You need to be mindful of where you step, alert for snakes, tree roots, and fire ants. Always be mindful of fire ants.

Birding is one of the few ways I can really be fully in the moment. I keep my focus on one goal: find and identify birds. With all my attention.

Someday I will do that in the rest of my life. Someday.

21

Hiding in Plain Site

Being mindful is a spiritual practice, but it is also a practical practice. If you pay full attention in each situation, will you gain spiritual wisdom, insight, and sense of calm. (So I am told.)

Mostly I go through life on auto-pilot, but I'm working on it. That is what this year is about. I know that the more I strive to pay attention and be mindful, the more I notice things I would have otherwise missed.

I have become more aware. I don't only see and hear what I expect. I notice what is there, hiding in plain sight. I pick up on the tone of my friend's voice. "I'm fine!" she says. But despite her words, I know she is absolutely not fine. Then I can act on the truth *behind* her words.

Tala taught me about the need to really see what is there, what might be hiding in plain sight.

Camouflage Dog

Tala tried to teach me this years ago.

I opened the door and whistle for Tala. She and her sister Olie each have their own unique call whistle. Tala knows her whistle. She knows when she hears it that she needs to come to me. She doesn't come.

I wait.

I whistle again, louder.

I look but I don't see her. I step out onto the porch. I call her name.

I scan the yard, but I don't see her. She could be behind the shed (in trouble no doubt) but usually she is really good about coming when I whistle. I'm stumped. I am about to put on my shoes and go looking for her.

Finally, I catch a hint of movement under the cherry tree in my direct line of site from the back door. I squint. (Does that really help?)

A breeze blows, moving the leaves and shifting the dappled shadows under the tree. I see her. My dappled blue-gray merle dog perfectly camouflaged in the shifting shadow and light under the trees. She is hiding in plain sight. Looking right at me. Waiting to see how long it will take me to notice her there.

"Really?!?" I say.

She gets up and walks to me, in no hurry and with a look of disdain. I can almost read her thoughts: "How did you get to be alpha?"

I look her in the eye and wiggle my thumb at her. "Opposable thumb. I can operate a corkscrew and open the wine bottle."

She trots happily inside having heard the word wine. Yes, she likes a sip or two. No, I don't give her more than that.

Don't judge me. I get enough judgement from her.

More Birding

As I shared in a previous chapter, birding is a mindfulness practice for me. It keeps me in the moment. But it also reminds me why being fully in each moment is important.

I know that I can't get the missed time back. I know that if I miss the experience, the emotions, of that moment, it is gone forever. I miss life, because life is moments.

I know, I am preaching to the choir. We all know that.

But if you are like me, knowledge doesn't change your daily behavior.

I listen to an audiobook while I clean. I totally defend this. I have tried full attention and even, heaven help me, expressing gratitude to my living space as I clean it as a sign of respect for its service to me. That didn't last long but it was an interesting experiment.

I listen to podcasts while I balance spreadsheets.

My grocery list plays in the background while I have a conversation with a neighbor.

My to do list is always running in the background of every interaction.

I should pay attention. I want to stay in the moment before the moment is gone. Honestly, I'm not that keen on having a conversation with my toilet as I scrub it. Don't get me wrong, I am a huge fan of indoor plumbing but I don't want to look back on my life and wonder where it went.

So I try to focus, to create those full attention moments.

Petting the dog. Holding a warm tea mug in my hands against the morning chill. But my mind is busy and it wanders off.

Birding demands more.

When birding, I can only focus on the one thing. See the bird. Pay attention to the shape of the bill, the way that it moves, the song it makes, its color and size. Take a few moments to enjoy watching a bit of nature. Identify the bird. Hopefully before it flies away. They do that.

Just like the moments of our lives

The Dandelion

It started with a dandelion. I escaped the office to get some fresh air. And there it was. The dandelion. It was perfectly shaped, in a full bloom of bright yellow, standing alone against a bright green background when it caught my eye.

My brain said "That is a weed."

My soul said "That is beautiful."

A few steps later, there was a moth resting on the ground. Its wings were a delicate filigree pattern of white on black. And again, my soul said "That is beautiful."

Then it became a challenge to see what I would normally overlook. "Let's see how much beauty I can find on this walk." Turns out despite my path through a parking lot next to a construction site, there was plenty of beauty to be noticed.

A clump of purple iris intentionally planted along the sidewalk's edge.

The sound of a woodpecker working high in the long leaf pine.

A wildflower, pink and self-effacing, turned away from me. So unlike the brash dandelion bursting out in the middle of the grass saying "look at me!"

My search for beauty was mindful. It was soothing to my computer-weary brain.

So I have added a new mindfulness practice: Seek out five (because I like that number) bits of beauty on my walks.

I already something similar when I walk Sandy. When walking Sandy, I see the ugly things that she might decide have an interesting smell. I am still mindful, but it's more defense.

Seeking beauty is more proactive. It is joyful.

My discovery of this practice wasn't planned, but perhaps the universe is taking pity on me for being so inept at this mindfulness thing.

Mindful Dog Walking

Walking a beagle requires full attention. That makes it a great mindfulness practice. I must stay in the moment. I must be fully present.

I see people at the park with their well-behaved dogs who never pull or randomly stop to examine a smell. The dog trots along beside the human who is usually scrolling through their phone. I envy these people with their busy social lives. They are getting messages from very important people. They don't have time to pay attention to their dogs or their neighbors or the flowers or anything that is not on that tiny screen.

Okay that's sarcasm and I don't envy them.

I think it is sad.

Walks with my dogs have always been about companionship. It is a way for us to bond and strengthen our pack. Every walk is a journey undertaken by the pack at the direction of the alpha (that's me.) My dogs follow my directions (mostly.) They offer their opinions about which trail to take or which spots to avoid. Ultimately I decide. That's my job.

It's sad to see a dog following her human, being a good pack member but getting nothing back. They don't get to socialize with other dogs or people, which is fine. Not all alphas want their pack to do that.

But these alphas aren't giving their dog any attention either. The dog is alone on the walk, but without the autonomy to go where they please. They get no reward for being a loyal pack member, no encouragement to keep being that loyal follower.

The humans are missing out too. They ignore their dog and miss out on the love and admiration their dog might have for them.

Walking Sandy keeps me on my toes. I have to scan for hazards: snakes, ground bees and fire ants. My dog is not the best behaved dog at the park. And I may not be the best alpha. But we are having fun and we are doing it together.

That's what counts.

Meditation

In 2019 I had a goal to create a daily meditation habit.

It went the way most New Year goals do: an overly ambitious start followed by a slow fade into obscurity as old habits creep back in.

Once or twice during the year guilt would get to me and I would revive the habit. For a few weeks I was calm and zen and pleased with myself. But then this day was busy. And the granddaughter slept over that day. And I'll do it later. Or tomorrow. Or next week. Or . . . never?

In short, a daily meditation habit didn't happen in 2019. But I promised myself, "2020 will be different."

I was right about that.

Not in the way I had hoped, but it was different.

Meditation should have been easier. I had more free time, there were no events, no parties, very little socializing. I am not a social butterfly but I know people and some of them like me and we do stuff together.

Except in 2020, we couldn't. My closest friends were either high-risk or lived with someone who was. My granddaughter was stressed over the loss of her school friends. Walks in the park were stressful for Sandy and people were reluctant to stop and pet her despite her best tail wagging efforts. And yes I was wearing a mask.

So, I had time on my hands. I tried to meditate. I really did.

My world was quieter. But my mind, my mind was loud and jumpy and scared. The year dragged on and the meditation did not happen. I hoped 2021 would be different.

I started a newsletter on mindfulness. That should hold me accountable for my habits including mediation, right?

Sort of. I found there are a lot of other ways to be mindful. Good to know.

But a learning about mindfulness is not being mindful. Learning is not sitting. Learning is not quietly breathing. It is not meditation.

So I'll start again – as soon as I run out of excuses. Right now, Sandy needs a walk.

Karmic Intervention

I am not happy with my inability to mediate. But I didn't have a solution for that yet. Until my old friend karma steps in.

I am waiting in the exam room at the dermatologist's office for my annual skin check. Sunny environment equals higher risk of skin cancer. So I stay ahead of the risk with this annual visit. I wait for the doctor. 5 minutes. 10 minutes. Sigh.

I can hear a conversation in the next room muffled by the wall. Beyond that are the barely discernable notes of a radio playing in the nurses station.

15 minutes

I'm bored. This exam room has plenty of posters on the wall. Mostly images of grotesque skin conditions. I avoid those and check out the before and after images of plastic surgery patients. I am not yet that vain.

There is a nice flat screen I could watch. It is rolling through informational graphics. Checklists of things to ask your doctor about. Pictures of grinning people whose horrible skin conditions were cured by miracle medications. Greetings from a friendly local pharmacy that would love to help me obtain those medications. No thank you.

20 minutes

I look to the opposite wall where a television (sound off) is tuned to a home remodeling show. A story of happy homeowners whose dreams are nearly dashed by hidden damage. Cured within the show's 30 minute run time, I am sure.

How long have I been waiting?

I do not want to think of all the projects I need to do at home or ponder the potential for hidden damage that I am blissfully unaware of. Will I have any money for such things when they are through with me here?

I should do something more productive with my time. I did not bring a book. I don't want to scroll Facebook on my phone. I could meditate. I mean, I'm not doing anything else. And the doctor does not seem to be in any hurry to interrupt my free time here.

So I sit up straight. Close my eyes. Breathe. Focus on my breath. Shut out the sounds from outside the room. Breathe.

I relax my shoulders. Breathe.

Imagine a golden light surrounding me. Feel that light. Breathe.

The tension leaves me. The answer to a question I was struggling with pops into my brain. Thank you. Breathe.

Hey! This stuff really works. So once again, I promise myself I will make time to meditate. Hopefully I mean it this time.

Yes, I finally did the see doctor. Everything was fine. My wallet is a little sore, though.

Lost

It is easy to get lost when hiking if the area is unfamiliar and everything looks the same. And if you are not mindful.

Sandy and I have gotten lost together. She was following her nose and I let her lead because I thought we were on the right trail. We weren't.

I stopped her. Considered the map in my mind and in my pocket. Looked around. No people. So we backtracked.

We found our way. We were tired and thirsty by the time we made our way back to the car, but we made it. And I learned. Don't trust only one sense and always take water – even on what is supposed to be a short hike.

Beagles get lost in the scents. Humans get lost in thoughts. Getting lost in your thoughts when hiking usually leads to getting lost in real life.

At least it has for me.

Of course, when realize you are lost, that will focus your attention in the present really fast. Unless you choose to berate yourself for your foolishness. Totally counterproductive.

You're lost.

It's time to find your way.

First stand still. Take stock. Make a plan.

Be mindful of your surroundings. Pay attention to the weather and the angle of the sun. You checked that before you started on the trail right?

You might use a compass. Or GPS. You might check a paper map. Use whatever resources you have at hand.

The same applies for getting lost in those repetitive thoughts.

Don't berate yourself. It happens.

Assess where you are. What you resources you have. And how you will use those to get back on track.

Just like a walk in the woods.

Halfway There

Suzanne's Mid-Year Update

I am halfway through this year of mindfulness experiment. I'd like to say it's going great and I am calmer, more centered and more in tune with my world. But that would be a lie. Still I persevere.

I have learned a few things. For starters, I have become aware of how unaware I am – that's progress right?

I did learn that:

Birding is a mindfulness practice.

I don't like super dark chocolate.

Sandy is not good at yoga.

Also, I am easily distracted and my brain is busy busy busy when I want it to be quiet.

I am doing better at sitting consistently to meditate. But not much better at actually staying focused on my breath. Busy brain! Still, I am putting this in the win column. I have to start somewhere and sitting is a start. It's the first command we teach a dog, right? So I am good at sit, but my brain won't stay.

Sandy's Mid-Year Update

Sandy is doing just fine because she is dog and dogs are always mindful. Sandy stays in tune with her world wherever she is. After all she doesn't want to miss a treat, or a new friend, or a new friend with a treat.

Perhaps one day, I will be as mindful as my dog. Until then, Sandy will be my guru, leading by example.

Walking an Old Dog

Lately on my outings with Sandy, I've been thinking about the difference between our hurry-to-the-smell walks and the walks I've taken in the past with other dogs. Dogs no longer with me. Ashes. Huff. Tala. Olie.

I believe that one of life's great privileges is walking an old dog. It might be a special sort of mindfulness practice.

Walking Olie

I love watching her tail wag when I get her leash. She doesn't leap up and run to me but her enthusiasm remains. I believe she enjoys the feel of a gentle breeze on her face as much as I do. I take real pleasure in the walk itself.

It's slow. It is not aerobic exercise, but that's okay. It's a chance to notice the things I would have missed at brisker pace with a younger full-energy dog.

I feel good because I am there, in that moment. Mindful.

I am strolling, not rushing. I have time to notice the flowers and the birds. I watch my beloved companion stretch her aging legs, hoping that keeps her moving longer.

I watching her sniff all the things. She enjoys the mental stimulation of the various sniffs to be found in the park. Her vision isn't so good. Her hearing is nearly gone. But her nose is still sensitive. Her wagging tail tells me she is happy.

I reminisce about her younger days when our walks were hurried. When there was so much to see and do. When her tail starts to droop, I know it is time to head back.

I am patient. Unusual for me. But I know that I can no longer can look forward to years of walks together. Time is running short. So I savor it.

Someday I know Sandy will be the old dog walking beside me. I'll be older too. And we'll both be okay with that. We will enjoy a slow more mindful walk. Together.

Visualization

I love visualization, not as a form of meditation, although some people use it that way. I use it as a stress reducer.

My recent travel plans provoked intense anxiety in me. I worry over all the plausible what ifs. This is not a bad thing, it is good to be prepared.

But then my brain creates more and more disastrous (although less likely) what-ifs. My brain can take a two-hour layover in the Atlanta airport, toss in a missed connection, and suddenly I am in an alternate future where I live out my days as a homeless person on the streets of Atlanta.

I mean, it could happen? Right?

I cannot make my brain stop imagining. So I direct it into more positive pathways.

Instead of burrowing deeper into implausible rabbit holes, I visualize everything going right.

What if I made all my travel connections?

What if the planes were on time?

What if I enjoyed a vigorous walk in the Atlanta airport and never became homeless?

All those things did happen on a recent trip, even my planes were on time. Not that everything was perfect. I totally should have spent more time visualizing the stopover hotel I stayed in. But whatever.

I can't say visualization was responsible for my good fortune. But it helped me chill out and enjoy my trip more.

Sandy Struggled

Sandy was not happy about my travel plans. There was a great deal of moping and drama when I pulled out my suitcase. Perhaps I triggered some old scary memories for her. If she could have joined me in my visualization practice.

But she survived the ordeal. Her second favorite human - my son - stayed with her. She was fed and she had companionship. I returned and all is right with the world again.

I will continue to use visualization in other areas of my life: goals that I want to achieve, the future I hope for. It will continue to be my go-to anxiety-buster.

Sandy will continue to use her emo-powers to induce guilt in me.

Visualization is not mindfulness since it takes you out of the present. Taoists often use it to ease into mediation conjuring images of healing light or serene energy. Zen followers consider this a distraction and strive for total clearing of the mind.

But if anxiety and an overactive imagination derail your attempts to meditate, perhaps visualization could be the back door into peace and serenity for you. Maybe even into mindfulness.

Pet the Dog

It should be easy to be mindful when petting a dog. They love the ear scritches and belly rubs. As they age, they prefer gentler strokes. It should be easy. Pet the dog is a good mantra.

Petting the dog is good for you too. Lowers blood pressure. Improves your mood.

I love Sandy. I talk to her while I pet her. But as she lulls into a restful state, my brain goes off the rails. It jumps around and I soon I forget that there is another being craving my attention. I start thinking about my to-do list or what I want for dinner.

Sandy is aware of the shift. She will get up and lay on the couch with her back to me. I have clearly offended her. Or she will find a toy and try to initiate a game of tug. Which I agree to, because I get it. I have been a neglectful human and need to pay attention.

This week I have tried to keep my focus on my dog. The to-do list can wait. And dinner will happen without obsessive pre-planning.

I pet the dog. I relax. I pet the dog. Nothing more.

It has been good for me. I feel calmer. Maybe I can do this mindfulness thing.

Hopefully this is a bonding experience for us. After my recent vacation, she needs a little extra love and reassurance.

Jaded

After you've been around a few years, you start to believe the adage that "there's nothing new under the sun."

You start to think there is nothing new to see. So you stop looking. In other words, you are jaded.

An attitude of mindfulness requires you to look. Even if you've seen it all before. Spoiler alert! You haven't.

Sadly, I am not at home to walk my pup each day at lunch. That will have to wait for retirement. Instead, I take the same walk at lunchtime each day. I leave my building and walk down a paved one lane road that leads to a dock over the intercoastal waterway. Nice.

The road is wooded on either side. There isn't much traffic and if there is a vehicle, it's usually someone I work with. So unless I've really irritated someone that day, I feel confident they will make an effort to drive carefully enough not to kill me.

The dock reaches out over a marsh complete with herons fishing and osprey (the birds not the helicopters) circling overhead. At low tide fiddler crabs scramble about in search of food. It smells like a marsh too: salty with just a hint of decay.

By the end of the dock the water is deeper, creating a channel for boats. During the summer, jet skis compete with the fisherman for space on the water. In the winter when the tide is right with fish running close to shore, the dolphins show up.

I've been here so many times, I don't expect to see anything new. But I still delight at the sight of dolphins and herons. I love the wave of the seagrass and the sound it makes as a boat's wake washes over it. It bends to the water as it must, but it springs back quickly unchanged. Very wise, that seagrass.

I don't expect to see anything new. But sometimes I do:

White pelicans too far north of their range, displaced by a hurricane south of here.

Flat topped deep blue-gray cumulonimbus clouds covering ¾ of horizon. I now know they are bringing a storm. (You live and learn.)

Oh yeah, and that snake. Big snake. Like I couldn't get my two hands around its girth big. (No, I did not try.) Its middle section was in the road but the ends were somewhere in the marsh-y woods. It was the sort of snake you see in videos and sort of wonder if they haven't somehow faked it. I was definitely mindful that day. My full attention was in the moment. Absolutely.

Don't become jaded. You never know when you will learn that you have not, in fact seen it all.

Stay mindful my friends.

Morning Mindfulness

I find it easy to be mindful when the world is waking up.

A walk at dawn keeps my brain in the here and now. Perhaps it is the quiet lack of distractions. Perhaps it is only my curiosity about what happens in my neighborhood before the humans come out.

When I can get out before the birds are singing, the world seems calm and fresh and hopeful.

Huff and I did a lot of those walks. He wasn't a fan of other dogs so we would get up early before the neighbors and their dogs were out and about.

We'd head out while it was still dark.

The early hour let us see things we would have missed. More than once we crossed paths with a fox contently trotting back home after a night out. He would glanced in our direction but didn't seem overly concerned.

We heard screech owls in winter. I came to love their graveyard sound call. But it wasn't until summer that we saw screech owlets lined up along the fence. Five of them. Huff wasn't so happy about that. Life had taught him to err on the side of caution. Personally I thought the babies were adorable.

Huff liked to sniff a bit, see who had been there before us – especially if it was a cat. He would have chased a cat. But it was too dark for his old eyes to see and while his nose told him something was there, he couldn't see it. That's okay. Chasing cats is a young dog's game.

We walked our route each day. Huff grazed on his favorite patch of grass in the spring when it first sprouted but never again until next spring.

In the same way that the first tomatoes of summer are delicious and the winter hot house ones are not worth the time, I guess.

By the time we completed the circuit of the neighborhood, it was light. The neighbors were walking or warming up cars to leave for work. It was once again a distracting place.

But the calm of my morning mindfulness remained.

Mindfulness vs Anxiety

In the war between the two, most often anxiety wins – in my life at least. This year of mindfulness is my attempt to change that.

Anxiety is about what is next, next minute, next hour, next week, month, year etc., etc.

Mindfulness is about now. Just now. If something bad is happening now, I deal with it.

If something might happen, I can't actually deal with it. I prepare for it – taking me back to week 1 when my anxious brain tried to convince me that mindfulness was shortsightedness. Resistance made a convincing argument: I would never get anything done if I didn't plan, or think, or worry.

With that word worry, I slipped into anxiety territory.

Which is the time to call in mindfulness. Time to acknowledge the bad stuff isn't now, it's merely a maybe.

Once I have done what I can, I need to relax. I need to breathe and breathe again. To meditate on here and now. To slow down and pet the dog. To get Sandy out and into the woods, hopefully on the right trail. To stay in the moment.

These are all things I have known for years, yet I still struggle.

The point of a mindfulness practice is to be ready when anxiety comes calling. To stay here in the moment and say "Thank you Anxiety, for trying to protect me. I'm as prepared for that as I can be. Now move along."

The Interrupter

I am an interrupter. (Hangs head shamefully)

I have the obnoxious habit of interrupting people when they are talking. I know better. I want to do better, I remind myself to do better. I berate myself when I fail. None of that works.

This week I am trying mindfulness.

I have come to see interrupting as a lack of mindfulness. When I cut in with my own thoughts, I am stepping out of the moment. I am ignoring the conversation that is happening in the present so that I can talk about something from my past or an idea for the future.

I am not mindful of the person speaking. I am not mindful of the value of their words and their thoughts. I let myself forget their value to me.

Granted some people must be interrupted or you will never get to speak. I don't spend a lot of time with such people.

In this practice, I am concerned with people who I care about. Who I want to know more about, yet my interruptions, my lack of mindfulness interfere.

Sometimes I am simply excited and I want to help. I want to share what I know but talking over someone is rude. Honestly, my friends can usually figure their own stuff out. Sometimes all they need is someone to listen or ask good questions.

Dogs Interrupt

Sandy interrupts me of course. Not with words. But any dog lover knows they interrupt in ways that can't be ignored.

This happens when:

I am talking too much and not petting her enough.

I am on the phone too long and we should be playing.

Other times, she interrupts when she feels my anxiety rising. She gets a toy or asks to go for walk. Interrupting in the very best way. Not for herself, but for her human. Okay, a little bit for herself.

I'm off to lunch with a friend now. Taking my mindfulness with me. Promising to listen, to ask good questions, and to only interrupt in the very best way, like Sandy.

I'll let you know how it goes!

The Interrupter Follow-up

Last week I resolved to stop interrupting. To interrupt my interruptions, so to speak. (Sorry I couldn't help myself.)

So how did it go?

Better than expected. I am actually learning. I still slip back into old habits, but not so often. I am improving and I call that a win.

Yes, I have a few times forgotten what I was going to say because I decided to listen instead. But the world did not end. My brilliant thoughts evaporated and yet no one suffered dire consequences from the loss of my wisdom. Huh. Go figure.

Difficult Lesson

I learned something disturbing. I learned that interrupting is an easy way to avoid the difficult conversations. It is a good defense mechanism.

To actually listen means to be fully engaged. That puts you at the mercy of what the other person wants to share. Perhaps the benefit of interrupting is that we can ignore the truth of the relationship.

Obviously, you don't have to care or respond or do anything merely because someone shared a particularly emotional bit of information. Except if I am listening to someone, it's because they matter to me.

Hearing what they were saying—and not saying—was sometimes difficult. I heard the fear or pain that the words were masking. I would have missed that if I had been preparing my response.

Benefits

I got more out of conversations. I understood more. I couldn't stay on the surface because I noticed too much.

Some relationships deepened and I feel closer to my friends.

On the other side, there were times when I heard the falseness of the words. The intent to deceive. This was valuable information. Painful, but valuable.

This practice has made me even more mindful (hooray!) of who I am choosing to engage with. It has also reinforced the importance of really listening.

Sandy of course is always here to listen to me. Unless it's time to walk. . .

Spiders

It's September. In the southern USA, it's Spider Season.

They are everywhere, building webs across walkways, tangled in playsets. There is even one who took over my hammock. With a little careful rearranging, we have managed a truce on that. She has one end of the hammock. I have the other. An uneasy truce.

I am not a big spider fan.

But I am even less a fan of the random bugs (looking at you mosquitos) that get trapped in a spider's web. So we formed an alliance. Not a warm fuzzy trust-y alliance but a practical eat-what-bites-me-and-I-will-share-my-hammock alliance.

The other morning Sandy and I headed to a local park. It has wooded trails, perfect for beating the heat. This time of year, it is also perfect for spiders. I hadn't thought of that.

My first clue was the walking stick leaning against the fence at the trailhead. It had no doubt been pressed into service as a web-clearing device. Then it was left there for the next traveler who would traverse the web-crossed trails. An act of kindness.

I took my own walking stick, leaving the tool for the next person, who might not keep a walking stick in the trunk of their car. How unprepared!

At the entrance to the trail, I looked up to see a huge web. In the center of that web is a rather large, probably not lethal to me spider. That confirmed my walking-stick-as-web-clearer hypothesis.

The giant web wasn't blocking the trail and I was on their turf. So I went under.

But I flailed my walking stick up and down and across in front of me as I walked. Sandy looked at me as if I had lost my mind.

Which I had. My goal had been to take a calming walk in the woods with my dog. To enjoy the trees and plants and birds. Mindful. Calm.

I didn't do any of that.

I was too busy trying not to walk into webs and failing several times. Then doing the ritual dance of: Where is it? Is it on me? Get this web off me!

Apparently we were the first ones on the trail that morning. You're welcome, everyone who came after us.

So my lovely morning mindfulness walk turned into a Halloween haunted house ritual. My morning mindfulness devolved into an elaborate dance of preemptive attacks and aerobic moments of panic.

I was in the moment, but not in a peaceful way.

Where You Are

The follow-up to my 'dances with spiders' walk was rewarding myself and Sandy with a treat from the local coffee shop drive through. Coffee for me. A dog treat for Sandy.

There was a line. I know they aren't fast. But it's the local coffee shop not the national chain, so I prefer to patronize them.

A major factor in that decision is the fact that the national chain does not have dog treats.

The local folks have a big plastic container of dog treats right by the pickup window. Sandy waits patiently in the back seat for a human to appear at the window. Then she sticks her nose out the car window with her best cute-puppy face and a madly wagging tail.

As soon as she hears the magic word *treat* (as in "Can your dog have a treat?") Sandy ducks back and plants her butt in the center of the back seat. This is the spot where she knows the treat will be delivered to her. It is the only place where I will give her the treat. I won't risk her jumping out to take the treat as it is passed to me.

Sandy is amazingly cooperative when there is a treat involved.

But before we get to the pickup window, we must wait. The drive through snakes around behind the building past the loading dock. There was one scraggly dogwood in a sickly patch of grass next to the building. Not picturesque.

We wait and we wait. I look around and notice a mockingbird using a low spot in the building gutter for a bird bath. His joy was infectious. He jumped in, splashed about. He jumped out shaking off. Preening. Then back in again. I was mesmerized. I was mindful. I was in the moment, paying attention.

The mindfulness I sought in the woods escaped me. I found it in the parking lot.

It's not where you are: it's what you notice.

Eventually the line moved. Sandy got her treat.

I got coffee, with a side of mindfulness.

Needing Mindfulness

I need mindfulness today.

Someone has hurt a person I love and I am powerless to intervene.

I tell myself karma.

I tell myself time is on my side.

I tell myself that anger leads to hate (almost there) and that hate will only hurt me.

That the perpetrator would feed off my anger and hate.

That they will never come around and it is time to write them off.

My obsessive thoughts only hurt me.

My obsessive thoughts keep me from checking in on my friends because they all have their own problems. I don't want to drag them down.

It is time for me to be still and wait.

It is time for me to remember to use what little power I have.

Even if that power is only the ability to sit and wait while the fire burns itself out. I will be touched by the flames but I will not be destroyed.

I will wait in this moment.

I will wait.

Obsessive Mindfulness

After spending 9 months (seriously you can grow a new human in this amount of time) striving for mindfulness, I find an article telling me that mindfulness can be bad for you.

Okay, granted you can find pretty much anything on the internet.

But they had some good points. Like mindfulness can be a form of overthinking (something I excel at.) This happens when the task you are performing is one you are already adept at. They give the example of athletes "choking" because they are too focused on the details of the task at hand.

Basically if you know how to do something, you don't need to overthink it. Focusing all your mindful powers on it will be counterproductive.

So where does that leave me and my quest for mindfulness?

In this case what the athletes need to do is clear their mind. (Ahem sounds like meditation.) They don't need to focus on the task, they need to relax and let it flow.

Since I am adept at very few things, I am probably safe from this problem. But if I ever find myself on a pro golf tour or taking a foul shot that could decide the game, I will try not to choke. On my laughter. Then I will wake up, because such a thing will not happen in my real life.

Screen Time

A stumbling block to my mindfulness is screen time.

I suffer from FOMO - that addictive feeling that there might be a cool blog post I haven't read yet. A friend may have shared pictures of her new puppy. Or maybe I got a text. I might have gotten a text. I need to check!

So I pick up my phone at 8:00 pm to see if someone texted me. Guess what? Nope.

Since the phone is in my hand, I check social media for cute dog pictures. Sandy is next to my on the couch and I could pet her. Instead, I scroll. Suddenly, it's past my bedtime. I've ignored my actual dog in favorite of pixels of dogs.

I have to rush around doing the evening chores, prepping for the next workday. Finally, I flop down in bed with my brain racing. Not restful. Not mindful.

My new goal is to avoid screens after 7:00 pm. I'm not sure what I will do with myself.

Pay attention to my family perhaps? Or meditate? I've struggled to find time for that. Maybe some gentle end of day yoga. All mindful things.

My phone is gonna miss me. But I bet my dog is happier.

Awareness

Three quarters of the way through the year and I'm still struggling with mindfulness. My biggest accomplishment this year is awareness: noticing when I am lost in the labyrinth of my brain. That is a mere baby step on the journey to Zen master mindfulness.

Fortunately, that was not my goal.

I was aiming higher. I was going for dog-level present moment awareness.

And falling way short.

I have three more months, and Sandy is helping.

Getting lost in the woods together forced me to pay more attention to my surroundings.

Our trip to the beach was an opportunity for me to focus on her delight at a brisk walk along the water's edge.

I can't wait to see what else she has in store for me.

Compassion Fatigue

We're all slogging through the pandemic. It's not over, but it feels like it should be. Maybe we're getting there. But maybe we're not a safe as we think. The uncertainty of it all drains our mental and emotional reserves.

We know that people are hurting – lost family members; lost livelihoods. We know the kids are suffering - disrupted schooling; fearful adults.

We are tired. Just tired of dealing with all the things, all the ways COVID has made life more complicated. We hate the way it has brought the fact of our vulnerability to us: right in our face, where we can't ignore it.

We just can't anymore. We can't deal with the mundane tasks of life. We can't care enough about others. This is compassion fatigue. We're not bad people. We are tired people.

Back in June, I hit that wall. I saw it coming but I pushed through, until I got sick and slammed into the wall. The proper metaphor is to lean on the wall and rest. But I didn't have sense enough to do that.

This is why dogs don't get burnout: they have sense enough to rest when they need to. except for working dogs prodded on by their humans. But most handlers are aware of their dog's needs and perhaps that awareness forces them to take the break they need as well. We need our four legged gurus!

But even hard working dogs rest when they get the chance. Herding dogs share tasks, work shifts.

Now when I feel the first tinges of compassion fatigue, I use mindfulness. This is one of the few times it is my go-to! Progress.

Here is my practice:

I stop thinking and look around. I see what is here now.

I listen. I hear the sounds that are here now.

I inhale deeply and pay attention to the scents around me, here now.

I give my mind the time to pay attention, to be where I am, here now.

I touch things. I connect with the here now through physical objects: the desk, a photograph (no not the digital kind), the squishy seal that my granddaughter gave me to deal with stress.

The practice works. (So does poking the squishy toy.)

This practice grounds me in the moment. This moment where the breeze is ruffling the maple leaves. This moment where a blue jay is squawking and air smells like it might rain. This moment when I remember my granddaughter loves me. And I love her. This moment. Here. Now.

I am mindful.

Courage

At the heart of mindfulness is courage. Being mindful means being here, being with whatever is happening now. That takes real courage.

In mindfulness you sit with the beauty; that's the easy part. Embracing the calming Zen-mood of mindfulness is not difficult.

But to be truly mindful, sometimes you sit with the ugly and painful, too.

The tears.

The empty spots that used to be full.

Mindfulness lets what is real emerge and have your attention. Real isn't always pretty. Sometimes real makes you angry. Sometimes real hurts.

You have to sit with the uncomfortable. If you are mindful, you will have to face what is really here:

the growing gap between you and a loved one.

the pain of a recent loss.

the labored breathing of a friend who claims there is nothing wrong, despite all those recent doctor appointments.

You do it all without projecting into the future. Or reliving the past.

You stay here, now. In the heart of mindfulness.

Acceptance

Last week I wrote about the times when mindfulness isn't all love and lightness. Sometimes, being in the moment is ugly and painful.

To be mindful you have to sit with whatever it is. Even when it's hard. Acknowledge what is. Keep breathing. Feel. Accept. Don't fight the moment. Move through it.

This is not to say I am particularly good at this. I prefer to rage against it. Or ignore it. Or distract myself. Anything but be still and be here.

This is why I am practicing. And, I actually I learned something. (That's the point after all!)

I learned that being mindful in the difficult moments is the way through those times. The quickest way through.

Once you let it wash over you, once you let it be, you can see it for what it is. You can move beyond resistance.

You are there with it. You stop resisting it.

Maybe you gain insight that lets you change it. (Hooray!)

Maybe you see it a different way. (Okay.)

Maybe there is nothing that can be done. (Well that stinks.)

But you no longer suffer because of it. Pain is unavoidable. Suffering is not. Suffering is fighting the pain.

Huff knew this. He was in a bad situation. He couldn't change it. He didn't fight it. He accepted things as they were. Because of that, when the moment came he recognized the opportunity for change. He grabbed the moment. He never looked back.

When you get a splinter you know removal will be painful. Maybe a lot, maybe only a little. You don't like it. But you accept it.

You don't suffer because you know the pain is the way forward. You know the consequences of ignoring the splinter is worse than the pain of the moment.

If you ignore it, the splinter will fester and that infection will last longer and bring more pain and you eventually still have to get the splinter out.

Mindfulness is not letting the painful ugly things in life fester. It is accepting

them and moving forward.

Huff knew about acceptance. It was his way out of a horrible situation. We can always learn from our four legged friends.

Fidget

I am by nature a fidget. I don't like to sit still. Calm is foreign to me but I try.

That is why I like walking meditations. It is why I find mindfulness in birding.

I can't sit still.

I'm sure I could get some meds, but I don't see this as a problem. No one in my life has complained.

I seem pretty functional, as far as I can tell.

Sandy approves of my walking habit. She is sure to remind me when I have been too long in human distractions. Starting with big sighs. Noisy shifts in her position on the bed. Finally getting up and nudging me. Reminding me that denying my fidgeting nature is not good and I really ought to walk the dog.

Mindfulness for physical health

If you are mindful, you don't just notice what's around you. You also notice you. Your body. Your feelings.

Humans are taught to ignore their emotions. We are told to "work through it" or "suck it up" when we are in physical pain. Many humans (although not this one) believe in "No pain. No gain."

Like my dogs, I believe we should be mindful of our pain. When my feelings are hurt, I don't like to focus on it. But I know I need to listen to it.

Likewise, I pay attention to what my body is trying to tell me. Both my body and emotions have valuable information I should not ignore.

A dog will never ignore pain. They will try to cover it up if they don't feel safe. In front of an enemy or an unknown, dog will pretend to be fine. A dog will walk on that leg that is really hurting.

I have seen my herding dog Huff tired, tail dropping as we finish up our walk. Then a strange dog approaches and he straightens up and pretends. We pass the other dog and once out of sight, Huff lets down his guard.

He knows he is safe with me. Once in the house, he flops down on his pillow. I massage his legs and comfort him. He makes no pretense that he is fine. He is hurting and he is not afraid to let me see that.

I do that too. I listen to my pain but I don't share it with everyone. I wait until I feel safe. Until I am safely back within my pack.

Sometimes we hide our pain so long, we convince ourselves it is not worth our attention.

But if we ignore our own pain, it will reemerge. It will come out in ways that hurt others. We snap. We growl. We push away the people who care about us.

This is what a stray dog will do. They will hide their injury. They will snap. They will growl. They will push away the very people who want to help them.

It's time for us to be mindful of ourselves. To look inside and acknowledge what's there. To be mindful.

That's the only way we can heal.

Holiday Crazy

We're all a little crazy now.

In October of 2021 we had the king tide, followed by the lunar eclipse. Add that to covid fatigue, add a dash of holiday anxiety and everyone seems a little on edge. It doesn't take much to push most of us over that edge.

You might find yourself overreacting even when part of your brain knows you are overreacting.

You might find yourself assuming the worst possible scenario even though you know that it is unlikely.

So as we work our way through the upcoming holidays, no matter what holidays you celebrate, keep in mind we need to be more like our dogs.

Dog Rules for Holidays

Greet everyone with enthusiasm.

Enjoy the treats: you can always go for an extra walk later.

Be kind. Be mindful that others are struggling with many of the same stressors.

Let's give each other a little more space and a little more slack.

When it's all too much, go walk the dog. Give yourself some space – and yes, give yourself a little more slack.

Surface Acting

Surface acting is science-speak for faking it. It is pretending things are fine, when they are not, in fact, fine. It is hiding your true emotions. Faking enthusiasm.

Dogs never do this. If they like you, you know it. If they don't, well you'll know that too.

The workplace is filled with surface acting. Sometimes it is absolutely necessary if you want to keep your job.

So how does it relate to mindfulness?

The more mindful you are, the harder it is to continue surface acting.

A study published *Journal of Applied Psychology* by Christopher J. Lyddy & colleagues concluded that "mindfulness can also amplify negative responses to aversive experiences."

In other words, when you are paying attention you don't ignore the bad stuff. You don't want to act anymore. You stop faking it. You express your true emotions.

Dogs Don't Fake It.

Dogs don't surface act. Ever. Even a dog who is abused by his owner will not fake emotions of love and admiration. He will obey out of necessity and fear, but he won't pretend he loves that owner.

If, like Huff, the dog gets a chance to escape, he will never look back.

The unwillingness to surface act is one reason behind what the media calls "The Great Resignation." It's more complicated than that, but the unwillingness to fake enthusiasm for soul sucking work is certainly a factor.

When the humans are done shuffling jobs and reorganizing the way society works, our dogs will still be here napping on the couch and waiting for the next walk.

Lunar Eclipse

In the early hours of In the early hours of 19th November, I roused myself from my comfy bed, bundled up and headed outside to watch the lunar eclipse.

I took my faithful companion Sandy with me. No, that's not true. When she saw my intention was to sit in one spot, outside in the cold and the dark with no snacks, she declined my invitation and went back to bed. Okay then.

I sat alone outside in the cold and dark as the bright full moon was swallowed up by the shadow of the earth.

I hadn't chosen this activity as a mindfulness practice, but it became one.

The movement was slow. The shift from light to dark was gradual.

I sat still, wishing I had made hot chocolate before getting comfortable. Obviously I still have work to do on this mindfulness thing.

As the sky darkened, other things become more visible.

At the umbra, when the moon was nearly obliterated, unseen stars become visible. The Pleiades star cluster, otherwise known as The Seven Sisters, magically appeared. Obviously, they had always been there. But they had been cloaked in light. Some things require darkness to be seen.

The planets rotated on. The Moon moved out of the earth's shadow. It grew brighter. The Pleiades faded in obscurity. I knew they were still there. But I could no longer see them.

The light did not erase my knowledge. Having seen them, I knew they were there, beyond my perception.

We often fear the dark, but it shows us other lights.

Holidays Alone

A good portion of the population spends their holiday alone.

Sometimes, I am part of that portion. The first time it happened I was devastated. I cried. I felt sorry for myself.

But once I got over my "it's not supposed to be like this," I was okay. Better than okay actually.

I went for a nice long walk on the uncrowded beach.

I cooked the dinner of my choice. I did not bother with a traditional holiday spread which would have been wasteful. Instead I made a normal meal and treated myself to a nice single size store bought dessert.

Then I settled in to watch a couple of good comedies. It was thoroughly enjoyable.

I was amazed. When I stopped feeling sorry for myself, I could be mindful. I could experience the good in the moment. There was a lot of good. Huh. Who knew?

My angst was merely an unfulfilled expectation. Years of spending holidays with family and friends had made me think it would always be that way. That it should be that way. That was never a given.

Whether you spend this holiday surrounded by loved ones or on your own, be mindful.

Accept what is and make it your own.

Solstice

This is my favorite holiday. Maybe because no one pays attention to it. It gets lost among all the celebrations of Christmas, Hanukkah, Festivus, New Year's Eve. This holiday sits tucked quietly away: the longest night of the year.

I like this night because it's quiet. No one expects me to dress up. I don't have to leave my house. There's no social pressure to participate in fun activities.

This night is a perfectly acceptable time to wear sweatpants and be alone with my dog. To reflect on all sorts of deep subjects. Or not.

Sandy does not like the dark. She is all for curling up into a warm ball once the sun sets. She knows this is a time to rest.

Tonight we will sit on the couch together. We'll share some snacks. I'll sip my glass of wine in the glow of the Christmas tree lights. I'll pet Sandy. She'll pretend to ignore me once the snacks are gone. But she will doze off, close by, her head resting against me. I am sure it is not all about the snacks.

Wrap up

After a year of this practice, I expected I would have mastered the art of mindfulness. Alas that was not to be.

I am better. But far short of mastery.

I have learned to pay attention to my body. I listen now to what it tells me, I notice when my shoulders tense up and creep toward my ears. I relax them.

I am making time every day – okay most days – to be mindful.

My big accomplishment is creating a habit of moments. Short bursts of mindfulness throughout my day.

I notice a beautiful weed while on my walk. I pause to watch the birds eating winter berries. I take a few extra moments to enjoy the warmth of Sandy's fur as I pet her.

I give myself these little gifts. I don't rush quite as much as I did a year ago. I give myself time to breath, to enjoy the moment.

I hope this habit continues. That's the point of a habit, right? It's automatic. You don't have to think about it. I want mindfulness to be that for me.

I will continue to make space for it and maybe it will spread and grow, becoming more and more until mindfulness becomes a default.

Sandy sighs as she waits for me to finish this book and get back to important things like walks and snacks. Mindfully of course!

Also by Suzanne Grosser

Healing For Life
Find Help: A PTSD Resource Guide
Quiet Courage: Conquering Fear and Despair with the Stockdale Paradox
Stay or Go: Loving or Leaving Someone with PTSD

Wisdom of Dogs
Mindfulness for Dog Lovers

Watch for more at https://www.wisdomofdogs.com/.

About the Author

The only thing I ever wanted to be when I grew up was a writer. (Except for a brief period when I was three years old and decided I would be a fire fighter because I really wanted to drive that fire engine.)

My parents read to me every day. Children's books, of course. But poetry and bits of the classics, too. Story time was my favorite part of the day.

Left alone to play, I enacted elaborate dramas with my stuffed animals. I told my dolls stories while I jumped on my bed. For some reason, the plot lines flowed better when I was jumping. (For the record I no longer do this. My knees are not as forgiving as they used to be.)

When I was five, I was so obsessed with stories, that I was even willing to give up my play time to go to school. My parents promised I would learn to read, so it seemed a fair deal. My plan was simple. Once I could read, I would not have to wait for someone else to read to me. Best of all, I could learn anything I needed or wanted to know. I figured I would not even have to go to school anymore. Brilliant!

That is when I learned that life does always follow your plan.

Read more at https://www.wisdomofdogs.com/.